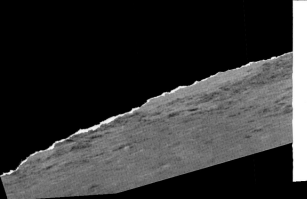

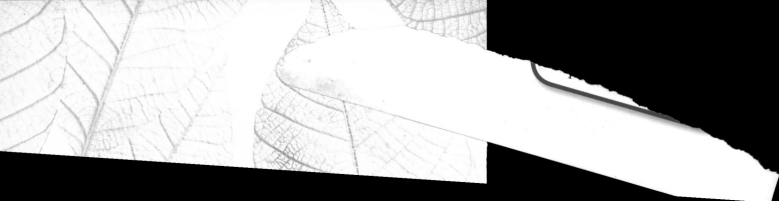

P. 52 "The voice carries out the work of the Buddha."

P. 59 "Three poisons" greed, anger + foolishness"

P. 53 "Practice + study arise from faith and faith is deepened by pursueing the 2 ways of practice + study."

FAITH,

PRACTICE,

AND STUDY

THE BASICS OF NICHIREN BUDDHISM

DAISAKU IKEDA

World Tribune
—Press—

Published by World Tribune Press
A division of the SGI-USA
606 Wilshire Blvd.
Santa Monica, CA 90401

Cover and interior design by Lightbourne, Inc.

22 21 20 19 18   1 2 3 4 5

ISBN: 978-1-944604-17-2

Library of Congress Control Number: 2018901450

Certified Chain of Custody
Promoting Sustainable Forestry
www.sfiprogram.org
SFI-01268

SUSTAINABLE FORESTRY INITIATIVE

SFI label applies to the text stock

CONTENTS

Editor's Note   vii

CHAPTER ONE   I

The Faith of the Soka Gakkai:
Unlocking Immeasurable Good Fortune and Benefit

CHAPTER TWO   19

The Practice of the Soka Gakkai:
Carrying Out Bodhisattva Practice in the Present Day

CHAPTER THREE   37

The Buddhist Study of the Soka Gakkai:
Elevating People's Life State

Notes   57

EDITOR'S NOTE

F aith, Practice, and Study: The Basics of Nichiren Buddhism is a
collection of essays by SGI President Ikeda in his series titled
"The Buddhism of the Sun—Illuminating the World," which
was published in Living Buddhism from June 2017 to August 2017.
The citations most commonly used in this book have been
abbreviated as follows:

GZ, page number(s) refers to the Gosho zenshu, the
Japanese-language compilation of letters, treatises, essays, and
oral teachings of Nichiren Daishonin.

LSOC, page number(s) refers to The Lotus Sutra and Its
Opening and Closing Sutras, translated by Burton Watson
(Tokyo: Soka Gakkai, 2009).

OTT, page number(s) refers to The Record of the Orally
Transmitted Teachings, translated by Burton Watson (Tokyo:
Soka Gakkai, 2004).

WND, page number(s) refers to The Writings of Nichiren
Daishonin, vol. 1 (WND-1) (Tokyo: Soka Gakkai, 1999) and vol.
2 (WND-2) (Tokyo: Soka Gakkai, 2006).

ONE

The Faith of the Soka Gakkai:

Unlocking Immeasurable Good Fortune and Benefit

On April 20, 1951, amid the ongoing postwar confusion and turmoil in Japanese society, the momentous first issue of the *Seikyo Shimbun,* the Soka Gakkai newspaper, was published. Today, sixty-five years and more than nineteen thousand issues later, the publication continues to impart hope and courage to its readers.

My mentor, second Soka Gakkai president Josei Toda, wanted people throughout Japan and around the world to read the *Seikyo Shimbun.* I share the same sentiment.

The written word is a powerful means for opening new frontiers for kosen-rufu. In particular, I will never forget the energy and passion that Mr. Toda poured into writing for the *Seikyo Shimbun* from its very first issue, including installments of his serialized novel *The Human Revolution,* a column titled "Epigrams," and other feature articles. He also wrote the main article that appeared on the front page of the paper's inaugural issue. It was titled "What Is Conviction?"

In it, he declared: "This is truly the time of kosen-rufu. We must be courageous."[1] To act with courage, he said, we must have absolute conviction in what we are doing.

At the time, Japanese society remained very chaotic. The Soka Gakkai still had only a small membership and had yet to become established in society. Nevertheless, Mr. Toda had absolute conviction, and that was why the Soka Gakkai was able to go on to achieve such phenomenal development.

Soka Gakkai Members Base Themselves on Faith, Practice, and Study

In his article on conviction, Mr. Toda stressed: "Faith, practice, and study are vital prerequisites for us followers of Nichiren Buddhism, and teaching others about the Mystic Law is an essential requirement for all believers who have pledged to realize kosen-rufu. Once we embrace the Gohonzon, we need to remember that the Buddha entrusted us with this mission countless ages in the past."[2]

Indeed, faith, practice, and study are the driving forces for the growth and victory of all SGI members, who are

Bodhisattvas of the Earth from time without beginning. They are eternal guidelines for our efforts to carry out the mission we have been entrusted by the Buddha.

In "The True Aspect of All Phenomena," Nichiren Daishonin writes: "Exert yourself in the two ways of practice and study. Without practice and study, there can be no Buddhism. You must not only persevere yourself; you must also teach others. Both practice and study arise from faith" (WND-1, 386).

Exerting ourselves in faith, practice, and study and upholding the correct teaching, directly connected to the Daishonin, have been the tradition of the Soka Gakkai since its earliest days. Today, Nichiren Buddhism pulses vibrantly only within the compassionate efforts of SGI members to propagate the Mystic Law based on faith, practice, and study.

At this time, when the SGI is making great strides as a world religion, I would like to reaffirm with our members everywhere the importance of faith, practice, and study by examining various passages from Nichiren's writings. In this chapter, let's focus on faith, the first of these basics of Nichiren Buddhism.

"We of the Soka Gakkai Have Faith"

This Gohonzon also is found only in the two characters for faith.[3] This is what the [Lotus Sutra] means when it states that one can "gain entrance through faith alone."

Since Nichiren's disciples and lay supporters believe solely in the Lotus Sutra, honestly discarding expedient means and not accepting even a single verse of the other sutras, exactly as the Lotus teaches, they can enter the treasure tower of the Gohonzon. How reassuring! Make every possible effort for the sake of your next life. What is most important is that, by chanting Nam-myoho-renge-kyo alone, you can attain Buddhahood. It will no doubt depend on the strength of your faith. To have faith is the basis of Buddhism. (WND-I, 832)

At a Soka Gakkai headquarters general meeting held in November 1957, as the accomplishment of his lifetime vow of achieving a membership of 750,000 households lay within sight, Mr. Toda declared, "We of the Soka Gakkai have faith."[4]

Many media representatives were present. Aware of their superficial speculations as to why the Soka Gakkai had developed so dramatically, Mr. Toda proclaimed unequivocally that we had won through faith. His lion's roar still rings in my ears.

He continued powerfully: "Faith is central! Our mission is practicing Nichiren Buddhism. As long as you remember that, you'll never be surprised by anything anyone writes or says about us."[5]

Faith means having the heart of a lion king, which allows us to overcome any adversity.

People with strong faith are not afraid of anything. As long as they have faith, unflagging conviction will well forth. Strong faith ensures a rich and fulfilling life. When we persevere in our practice of Nichiren Buddhism, we cannot fail to attain happiness and victory in life.

Through his speech at the general meeting, Mr. Toda called on Soka Gakkai members to remain undisturbed by the vagaries of public opinion and be prepared to advance based on faith.

Faith is our foundation and starting point—this is the essence of Nichiren Buddhism.

"The Gohonzon Is Found Only in Faith"

In "The Real Aspect of the Gohonzon," Nichiren explains the meaning of faith and the benefits that can be obtained through faith. He sent this letter to the lay nun Nichinyo to thank her for sending offerings dedicated to the Gohonzon.

In the letter, he explains that he inscribed the Gohonzon,

the object of devotion, as the "banner of propagation of the Lotus Sutra" (WND-1, 831). He calls it "the great mandala never before known" (WND-1, 832), with the power to enable all people to attain enlightenment, and "a cluster of blessings" (WND-1, 832), a source of infinite benefits.

This great Gohonzon, he states, is found only in faith.

Faith is the ultimate way to attain Buddhahood. The Lotus Sutra states that we "gain entrance through faith alone" (LSOC, 110). Even Shariputra, one of Shakyamuni's ten major disciples, who was hailed as "foremost in wisdom," could enter the boundless realm of Buddhahood only through faith, not through wisdom.

Similarly, even if the Gohonzon is right in front of us, without faith, we cannot bring forth its power.

Nichiren attained the life state of Buddhahood by persevering in his great struggle with the spirit of "single-mindedly desiring to see the Buddha, not hesitating even if it costs them their lives" (LSOC, 271).[6] He then inscribed his enlightened state of life in the form of a mandala—the Gohonzon. Through faith based on a deep awareness that the Gohonzon "exists only within the mortal flesh of us ordinary people who . . . chant Nam-myoho-renge-kyo" (WND-1, 832), we can bring forth immeasurable benefit.

When we summon forth the power of faith and practice, chant wholeheartedly to the Gohonzon, and dedicate ourselves to realizing the great vow for kosen-rufu, we can reveal the world of Buddhahood within us that is one with the Mystic

Law, manifest the power of the Buddha and the Law, and freely enjoy and make use of great benefits.

On this subject, Mr. Toda said: "When we muster the power of faith and the power of practice to a factor of one, it gives rise to the power of the Law and the power of the Buddha to the same factor. Similarly, a factor of one hundred yields a response of one hundred; a factor of ten thousand produces a reaction of ten thousand."[7]

Everything hinges on our faith. As the Daishonin states in a letter to another of his disciples, the lay nun Nichigon, "Whether or not your prayer is answered will depend on your faith; [if it is not] I will in no way be to blame" (WND-1, 1079).

People of strong faith never stagnate or reach an impasse.

Those who persevere in faith will experience the wonder of realizing within their own lives the same vast life state of Buddhahood attained by the Daishonin and be able to move everything in the direction of happiness.

Those who "gain entrance through faith alone" will never be defeated by misfortune.

Believing Solely in the Lotus Sutra Leads Directly to Happiness

Next, in above passage, Nichiren quotes two passages from the Lotus Sutra—"honestly discarding expedient means" (LSOC, 79) and "not accepting a single verse of the other sutras" (LSOC, 115). He does this to underscore how important it is to "believe solely" in the Lotus Sutra. "Solely," here, can also be interpreted to mean "as the one and only" as well as "single-mindedly."

Through solely believing in the Lotus Sutra, he says, one "can enter the treasure tower of the Gohonzon." In other words, through upholding the Gohonzon of Nam-myoho-renge-kyo and wholeheartedly dedicating ourselves to kosen-rufu, we can enter the palace of happiness that is the world of Buddhahood, wherever we are and whatever our circumstances.

Speaking of our attitude toward the Gohonzon, Mr. Toda said we should chant with single-minded faith, that is, believing solely in the Mystic Law.

By persevering with such faith, we can accrue immeasurable benefits. Through embracing the Mystic Law and striving earnestly in Buddhist practice, anyone can proudly walk the great path of human revolution, of absolute happiness.

Nichiren continues in this letter: "What is most important is that, by chanting Nam-myoho-renge-kyo alone, you can attain Buddhahood. It will no doubt depend on the strength of your faith."

Our happiness isn't decided by the length of time we have practiced Nichiren Buddhism—much less our position in the organization or in society. It's determined by the strength or depth of our faith.

A basic tenet of Nichiren Buddhism is that everything starts with faith, no matter who we are or what our circumstances.

"Winter Always Turns to Spring"

What is called faith is nothing unusual. Faith means putting one's trust in the Lotus Sutra, Shakyamuni, Many Treasures, the Buddhas and bodhisattvas of the ten directions, and the heavenly gods and benevolent deities, and chanting Nam-myoho-renge-kyo as a woman cherishes her husband, as a man lays down his life for his wife, as parents refuse to abandon their children, or as a child refuses to leave its mother.

Not only that, but one should ponder the sutra passages "Honestly discarding expedient means"[8] and "Not accepting a single verse of the other sutras"[9] without the slightest thought of casting them away, as a woman refuses to part with her mirror, or as a man wears his sword. (WND-I, 1036)

In this letter, "The Meaning of Faith" addressed to the lay nun Myoichi, Nichiren explains important aspects of faith that we should pay attention to.

Myoichi practiced Nichiren's teachings with her husband. Amid the oppression directed at Nichiren's followers after the Tatsunokuchi Persecution,[10] however, the couple had their land confiscated because of their faith. Then Myoichi's husband died before Nichiren was pardoned and allowed to return from exile on Sado Island.

Myoichi was left alone to raise two children, one of whom was ill. She herself was also in poor health. But she refused to be defeated by her trying circumstances and continued to fervently practice the Daishonin's teachings even after her husband's death. Despite her difficult economic situation, she supported Nichiren by sending a servant to assist him while he was on Sado and also later at Mount Minobu.

It was to this sincere "mother of kosen-rufu" that Nichiren sent his immortal message of hope: "Winter always turns to spring" (WND-1, 536). How these words of encouragement from her mentor must have inspired and sustained her!

Those who have suffered the most deserve to become the happiest people of all—this is the spirit of the truly empowering teachings of Nichiren Buddhism. It is the very heart of Nichiren Daishonin and the great humanistic philosophy of the Soka Gakkai.

Expressing Our Genuine, Unadorned Humanity

Later, Nichiren sent the lay nun Myoichi the letter titled "The Meaning of Faith." It opens with the words "What is called faith is nothing unusual."

To clarify his point, the Daishonin likens faith to the way a woman cherishes her husband, a man treasures and protects his wife, parents care for their children, and a child clings to its mother.

The affection between husband and wife or parent and child is a spontaneous expression of life, a natural manifestation of our inherent humanity. We should chant Nam-myoho-renge-kyo to the Gohonzon in the same unaffected, openhearted way. That is faith, the Daishonin says.

After being widowed, Myoichi continued to strive earnestly in faith, not only for herself but also for her departed husband, while doing her best to raise their children to be fine young people. No doubt the Daishonin's compassionate words resonated deeply in her heart.

Faith should always be honest and unpretentious.

As Nichiren writes: "Suffer what there is to suffer, enjoy what there is to enjoy. Regard both suffering and joy as facts of life, and continue chanting Nam-myoho-renge-kyo, no matter what happens" (WND-1, 681).

Whether experiencing suffering or joy, we should just take everything to the Gohonzon, expressing whatever is in our hearts as we chant.

Practicing Freely and Naturally

Nichiren inscribed the Gohonzon for the happiness of all people. When we chant Nam-myoho-renge-kyo to the Gohonzon and connect with Nichiren's enlightened life state embodied therein, we cannot fail to become happy. The Buddha of the Latter Day of the Law[11] assures protection for those who take action as his emissaries to advance kosen-rufu.

Strength or depth of faith cannot be measured by superficial markers. For example, Nichiren does not specifically instruct us on how long we should chant, and so on. Of course, it's important that we set personal targets for the amount we want to chant. That doesn't mean, however, that we should overdo things and force ourselves to chant when we are too tired or sleepy to do so, just because of some arbitrary quota we've set for ourselves. It might be more productive and valuable if we get some rest and chant the next morning, when we are refreshed in mind and body.

Nichiren also teaches that chanting Nam-myoho-renge-kyo even once has immeasurable benefit.

Elsewhere, he writes, "The neighing of the white horses [that revitalizes King Rinda] is the sound of our voices chanting Nam-myoho-renge-kyo"[12] (WND-1, 989). Let's bring forth powerful life force by chanting vibrantly and refreshingly with the rhythm of a magnificent steed galloping across the open plains.

Please remember that we are practicing this Buddhism to realize happiness for ourselves and others.

Vanquishing Fundamental Ignorance
by Being "Without Doubt"

The accepting and upholding of this original Law [Nam-myoho-renge-kyo] is expressed in the single word "belief" or "faith." The single word "belief" is the sharp sword with which one confronts and overcomes fundamental darkness or ignorance. The commentary [T'ien-t'ai's *Words and Phrases of the Lotus Sutra*] says, "Belief means to be without doubt." You should think about this. (OTT, 119–20)

There is one more important point regarding our attitude in faith, and that is believing without doubt.

In *The Record of the Orally Transmitted Teachings,* Nichiren says that faith is the "sharp sword" for vanquishing the deep-seated delusion of fundamental ignorance. To explain what faith is, he cites the definition given by T'ien-t'ai in his *Words and Phrases of the Lotus Sutra:* "Belief means to be without doubt."

"To be without doubt" means to believe in the Gohonzon with absolute faith, unshaken by any obstacle.

This is in contrast to understanding the teachings but lacking faith. Nichiren warns: "'Knowledge without faith' describes those who are knowledgeable about the Buddhist doctrines but have no faith. These people will never attain Buddhahood" (WND-1, 1030). Even if one can understand difficult Buddhist teachings intellectually, it will not be enough to attain Buddhahood in this lifetime.

What, then, does it mean to "be without doubt"? It is to believe wholeheartedly, to have absolute conviction. However, I should point out that there is a crucial distinction between being without doubt and simply never doubting.

If religion were to reject having doubts, it would be rejecting the inherent freedom of the human spirit. Such a religion would become alienated from society and run the risk of becoming dogmatic and fanatical.

Faith for Building an Unshakable Self

I embarked on the path of faith when I was nineteen. Although Mr. Toda had only just met me, he offered clear answers to each of my honest questions. His words rang with an unassailable wisdom and humanity. Later, I learned he had held fast to his beliefs even when imprisoned by the wartime militarist authorities.

I intuitively sensed that I could believe what this man said, and I decided to join the Soka Gakkai. Through first putting my faith in Mr. Toda as my mentor, I came to deepen my faith in the Mystic Law and the Gohonzon.

Naturally, as a youth who was new to the practice of Nichiren Buddhism, I had many questions. But having met Mr. Toda, I spent my days deeply pondering and reflecting on Buddhism's answers to the fundamental questions of existence and philosophy.

Mr. Toda often said: "Faith seeks understanding, and understanding deepens faith." *Understanding*, here, could also be expressed as "logic" or "reason." From my personal experience, faith is deepened by clarifying questions or doubts and continuing to think about them intently in the course of our Buddhist practice, until we finally arrive at a satisfactory answer that we can accept with all our hearts.

In *The Record of the Orally Transmitted Teachings,* Nichiren says, "Outside of belief there can be no understanding, and outside of understanding there can be no belief" (OTT, 54–55).

In other words, through deepening our faith, a seeking spirit to understand the teachings arises, and through studying the teachings and putting them into practice, we strengthen our conviction as we experience the power of Buddhist practice. Forging such absolute conviction in the depths of our lives is what it means "to be without doubt."

To return to the passage we are studying, Nichiren declares that fundamental ignorance can be vanquished with the "sharp sword" of faith—in other words, belief that is free of doubt.

Fundamental ignorance is the most basic kind of delusion or negativity—the inability to believe that the Buddha nature is inherent within our own lives. It is essentially tantamount to not being able to believe in the dignity of our own lives. If we cannot believe in our own Buddha nature, it naturally follows that we won't be able to believe in the Buddha nature of others either.

Science and technology, however advanced they may become, cannot solve this problem. In today's world, where mistrust and hatred are all too prevalent, Nichiren Buddhism teaches us how to make the supremely noble life state inherent within us shine forth, help others do the same, and create a life of true joy. Faith in the Mystic Law is the "sharp sword" that conquers the fundamental ignorance inherent in life.

"Nam-myoho-renge-kyo Is Your Own Life"

Mr. Toda asserted, "You have to be resolved that Nam-myoho-renge-kyo is your own life!"[13] and "Propagating the Mystic Law in the Latter Day means firmly believing that your life is nothing other than Nam-myoho-renge-kyo!"[14]

This is the conclusion of Nichiren Buddhism. I am convinced that Mr. Toda's words embody the unshakable conviction that is the very essence of the "sharp sword" of faith capable of dispelling all darkness or ignorance.

By practicing Nichiren Buddhism, we as SGI members can attain a state of life where we deeply perceive that we ourselves are entities of the Mystic Law, that each one of us possesses unlimited potential.

Kosen-rufu is nothing other than building, through a

spiritual revolution, an age in which each person acts based on a deep belief in the infinitely noble Buddha nature inherent in all people. We are spearheading this movement to effect a great change in the destiny of all humankind.

As SGI members, we are exerting ourselves in faith dedicated to the realization of kosen-rufu, aiming for the happiness of ourselves and others. This is the perfect embodiment of the all-important spirit of faith taught by Nichiren.

Many leading thinkers have expressed wonder and admiration for the rich experiences shared by our members everywhere—experiences gained through their Buddhist faith and practice.

Nichiren Daishonin writes, "Although I and my disciples may encounter various difficulties, if we do not harbor doubts in our hearts, we will as a matter of course attain Buddhahood" (WND-1, 283). The SGI is a gathering of champions who have internalized this passage. Undefeated by any hardship, our members have accumulated one experience of invincible faith after another. They have amassed boundless "treasures of the heart" and vastly deepened their faith. They have forged faith that is pure, deep, and strong.

The faith of SGI members is imbued with wisdom to live based on the ultimate truth of the Mystic Law, the courage to eradicate every form of misery, and the compassion that brims with the conviction that all people are Buddhas. Their faith is firmly established, enabling them to attain a life state of eternal happiness.

The Soka Gakkai Is Forever
an Organization of Faith

As SGI members, we have a pure commitment to truth and justice. We have firm conviction based on clear documentary, theoretical, and actual proof. We have a powerful and invincible belief.

The Soka Gakkai is forever an organization of faith.

Please join me, together with fellow members around the world, in proudly and confidently walking the great path of faith—united in the spirit of the oneness of mentor and disciple and directly connected to Nichiren Daishonin.

Now is the time to build an eternal foundation for the Soka Gakkai.

TWO

The Practice of the Soka Gakkai:

Carrying Out Bodhisattva Practice in the Present Day

Mahatma Gandhi, the leader of the Indian independence movement, was once asked what his religion was. Turning his gaze to the two sick people resting in his room, Gandhi replied, "To serve is my religion."[15] Religion to Gandhi meant serving the suffering people in front of him.

Like Gandhi, SGI members are demonstrating the true meaning of religion through their actions each day.

Creating an Age in Which Religion Serves Human Beings

Nichiren Buddhism is a quintessentially humanistic religion. It teaches that the most important priority is helping those who are suffering right in front of us and guiding them toward happiness.

The true worth of religion is found in reaching out to help those who are suffering or struggling, in actions of compassionate service to others. The difference between a religion that puts people first and a religion that exploits people for its own ends is simply whether it makes efforts to help people become happy.

In that respect, I believe, the bodhisattva practice taught in Buddhism can play an important role in determining the direction of religion in the twenty-first century.

On October 2, 1960, I took my first step for worldwide kosen-rufu.[16] Right from the start, I didn't do anything special. On each journey for kosen-rufu, I simply encouraged each person I met. I have encouraged countless individuals, always treating the person in front of me with the utmost respect and compassion.

Sharing my spirit, our members around the world are doing the same. Some regularly travel five or six hours, half a day, even a whole day, just to meet with a single person who needs their support. These steady, persevering efforts to establish human bonds based on encouragement are what have built today's global SGI network.

People all around the world express their admiration for this modern-day bodhisattva practice of SGI members. The age has come when people everywhere are eagerly seeking the philosophy and ideals of the SGI.

Core to our bodhisattva practice is practice for ourselves and practice for others. This encompasses both Buddhist practice for our own human revolution as well as efforts to expand the movement of kosen-rufu.

In this chapter, let us explore the element of practice.

A Call to Be Active
Practitioners of Buddhism

A mind now clouded by the illusions of the innate darkness of life is like a tarnished mirror, but when polished, it is sure to become like a clear mirror, reflecting the essential nature of phenomena and the true aspect of reality. Arouse deep faith, and diligently polish your mirror day and night. How should you polish it? Only by chanting Nam-myoho-renge-kyo. (WND-1, 4)[17]

Founding Soka Gakkai president Tsunesaburo Makiguchi gave a lecture titled "Believers, Practitioners, and Scholars of the Lotus Sutra and Methods of Investigation." In it, he urged:

We must clearly distinguish between believers and practitioners. While a person will surely gain benefit simply by having faith and offering prayers, this alone does not constitute bodhisattva practice. There is no such thing as a self-centered Buddha who only accumulates personal benefit and does not work for the well-being of others. Unless we carry out bodhisattva practice, we cannot attain Buddhahood.[18]

This short statement contains the essence of the faith of the Soka Gakkai.

It isn't enough to simply have faith and be a believer. It isn't enough just to study and be a scholar of Buddhism. We cannot truly understand Buddhism unless we are practitioners who take action for the happiness of others.

Mr. Makiguchi declared that Soka Gakkai members are people of actual practice—in other words, they are practitioners of the Lotus Sutra in the Latter Day of the Law and genuine Buddhists carrying out bodhisattva practice.

As SGI members, we uphold faith in the Gohonzon and exert ourselves in Buddhist practice every day. This Buddhist practice consists of both practice for ourselves and practice for others. Such efforts enable us to reveal our inner Buddhahood and attain a state of absolute happiness and help others do the same.

Practice for ourselves means efforts for our personal benefit and specifically refers to our daily practice of gongyo—reciting excerpts of the Lotus Sutra and chanting Nam-myoho-renge-kyo. Practice for others means efforts we make so that others can also receive benefit and specifically refers to teaching others about Nichiren Buddhism and spreading the Mystic Law. All our various activities for kosen-rufu, no matter how modest, constitute practice for others.

As Nichiren writes, "You must not only persevere yourself; you must also teach others" (WND-1, 386). Our efforts for the happiness of ourselves and others, Mr. Makiguchi taught, are crucial as practitioners of the Lotus Sutra.

The Practice for Transforming Our State of Life

The above passage from "On Attaining Buddhahood in This Lifetime" explains the function of chanting Nam-myoho-renge-kyo, the concrete practice for transforming our state of life. Mr. Makiguchi underlined this passage in his personal copy of Nichiren's writings.

Nichiren inscribed the Gohonzon and established the practice of chanting Nam-myoho-renge-kyo to enable all people to attain Buddhahood. He created a universally accessible form of Buddhist practice. This was indeed a great religious revolution.

Nichiren Buddhism underscores the importance of transforming our minds, our fundamental mind-set. Generally, people tend to think there is a huge divide between ordinary people and Buddhas. But Nichiren taught that there is no such gap—the only difference is that of being deluded and being awakened. Chanting Nam-myoho-renge-kyo is the means for transforming a deluded state of life into an enlightened one.

In this passage, the Daishonin likens a life of suffering, shrouded in fundamental ignorance,[19] to a tarnished mirror, and a life awakened to the truth of reality to a clear mirror. A tarnished mirror that doesn't reflect anything can become clear when it is polished, revealing all things.

Similarly, by continuing to earnestly chant Nam-myoho-renge-kyo, we refine our lives and clear away ignorance and delusion. We bring forth from within us the vast life state and wisdom of the Buddha.

Through our daily practice of gongyo, we polish and transform our state of life.

The above passage cites the requirements for this. First, we must "arouse deep faith," and second, we must "diligently polish" our mirror "day and night."

To combat the fundamental delusion obstructing our attainment of enlightenment, we need the courage to summon up deep faith. Also, if we are to attain Buddhahood in this lifetime, it's vital that we maintain our faith, diligently persisting in our efforts. Maintaining faith means never regressing.

In many places, Nichiren stresses the importance of striving with unwavering faith. For example:

One . . . who chants the daimoku [Nam-myoho-renge-kyo] is the Thus Come One's emissary. Also, one who perseveres through great persecutions and embraces

24

the [Lotus Sutra] from beginning to end is the Thus Come One's emissary. (WND-1, 942)

Carry through with your faith in the Lotus Sutra. You cannot strike fire from flint if you stop halfway. (WND-1, 319)

Achieving Lives in Which We "Enjoy Ourselves at Ease"

The aim of our Buddhist practice is to secure a state of happiness in which we "enjoy ourselves at ease" [see LSOC, 272].[20]

Elsewhere, Nichiren clearly writes, "There is no true happiness for human beings other than chanting Nam-myoho-renge-kyo" (WND-1, 681).

No matter how difficult the challenges we face, we will remain undefeated if we bring forth our inner Buddhahood through chanting Nam-myoho-renge-kyo. With the power of Nam-myoho-renge-kyo, which is like a lion's roar, we can triumph over all and lead lives in which we "enjoy ourselves at ease." We can transform lives of despair over our fate into joyful lives of mission in which we encourage and help others. Countless SGI members have advanced cheerfully with this conviction, demonstrating this truth in their lives.

None are more admirable than our members who strive as practitioners of the Lotus Sutra for their own and others' happiness.

My mentor, Mr. Toda, said: "No matter what happens, you can win by chanting Nam-myoho-renge-kyo. You can change hardship into strength, reveal your Buddhahood, and shape your own destiny. Just as you are, you can help all kinds of people become happy."

Our practice of chanting Nam-myoho-renge-kyo as practitioners of the Lotus Sutra enables us to not only lead lives in which we "enjoy ourselves at ease" but also to help others do the same.

"Propagation Is the Lifeblood of Religion"

Those who become Nichiren's disciples and lay believers should realize the profound karmic relationship they share with him and spread the Lotus Sutra as he does. Being known as a votary of the Lotus Sutra is a bitter, yet unavoidable, destiny. (WND-1, 994)[21]

The next passage we will study is from "Letter to Jakunichi-bo," in which the Daishonin urges his disciples to awaken to their mission as practitioners of the Lotus Sutra—that is, as Bodhisattvas of the Earth—and spread the Lotus Sutra as he did.

The mission of practitioners of the Lotus Sutra is to engage in practice for oneself and others in this evil age of the Latter Day of the Law, making wholehearted efforts to lead one person after another to enlightenment.

Propagating Buddhism in the Latter Day is a great and noble undertaking to overcome the three poisons of greed, anger, and foolishness[22] and transform the destiny of humanity.

In the spring of 1939, Mr. Makiguchi traveled to Yame in Fukuoka Prefecture, Kyushu, to share Nichiren teachings with the sister-in-law of a member in Tokyo. The woman decided to take faith, and the very next day, Mr. Makiguchi said, "Let's put our faith into practice!" He then set out with her and her husband, who had already decided to start practicing a short time earlier, to visit the home of a couple he knew in Unzen, in neighboring Nagasaki Prefecture, to introduce them to Nichiren Buddhism.

On that occasion, Mr. Makiguchi resolutely declared, "Propagation is the lifeblood of religion." And these words became the starting point of the movement for kosen-rufu in Kyushu.

Only through putting its teachings into practice can we experience the true greatness of Buddhism. Action is the lifeline of practitioners of Nichiren Buddhism. Mr. Makiguchi demonstrated this truth through his own example.

Living the "Encouraging Devotion" Chapter of the Lotus Sutra

In "Letter to Jakunichi-bo," prior to the passage we are studying, Nichiren writes: "Nichiren is the supreme votary of the Lotus Sutra in Japan. In this land only he has lived the twenty-line verse[23] of the 'Encouraging Devotion' chapter" (WND-I, 993).

The verse he refers to here is the concluding section of the "Encouraging Devotion" chapter of the Lotus Sutra, which states that persecution by the three powerful enemies— arrogant lay people, arrogant priests, and arrogant false sages—will befall those who spread the Mystic Law in the evil age after the Buddha's passing.

He also says that he has stood up with the awareness of fulfilling the mission of Bodhisattva Superior Practices[24] and urged the people of Japan to accept and uphold the Lotus Sutra, adding that he has not slackened in his efforts even after taking up residence on Mount Minobu.[25]

And in the passage we are studying, he says that his disciples should follow his example, spreading the Lotus Sutra as he does and steadfastly striving to lead people to enlightenment in accord with the Lotus Sutra's spirit of widespread propagation.

28

A "Profound Karmic Relationship"

The Daishonin writes of the "profound karmic relationship" that his disciples share with him, that is, the bonds connecting them from past existences. Nichiren often writes of the karmic ties he and his disciples share. For example:

> It must be ties of karma from the distant past that have destined you to become my disciple at a time like this. (WND-1, 217)

> A bond of karma from the past has led you to become my disciple. (WND-1, 387)

> You should realize that it is because of a profound karmic relationship from the past that you can teach others even a sentence or phrase of the Lotus Sutra. (WND-1, 33)

Disciples who have a "profound karmic relationship" with the Daishonin could also be described as disciples who strive alongside him. There is no greater honor than leading lives in which we share a struggle with the mentor in the effort for kosen-rufu.

The earlier passage ends with "Being known as a votary of the Lotus Sutra is a bitter, yet unavoidable, destiny."

In other words, in the eyes of the world, becoming Nichiren's disciple and suffering persecution because of one's commitment to the Lotus Sutra is a misfortune, a calamity. But when we view the depth of that karmic relationship from the perspective of Buddhism, there is no greater happiness than being able to work for kosen-rufu as a Bodhisattva of the Earth in the same spirit as Nichiren. Meeting with obstacles in the course of our efforts to spread the Mystic Law is an inevitable honor we encounter, which is why we need to stand firm with resolute faith.

We are committed to sharing Buddhism with all those with whom we have a connection, in exact accord with Nichiren's direction that we "spread the Lotus Sutra as he does" (WND-1, 994).

Having been born into this world, we dedicate ourselves to the happiness of others and lead lives contributing to society, earning the appreciation of countless people for our efforts to help them. This is the most worthwhile way of life possible for a human being.

Our efforts to sow the seeds of Buddhahood sometimes produce quick results and sometimes require time before results appear, but the benefits are the same in either case.

THE PRACTICE OF THE SOKA GAKKAI

Whether those we talk with start practicing immediately, the important thing is that we do our best to share Buddhism with them, sincerely and confidently, and that we make persistent, wholehearted efforts to help them understand the teachings. If we can achieve that, the seeds of Buddhahood we sow in their hearts are certain to eventually sprout and grow.

Elsewhere Nichiren writes, "Chant Nam-myoho-renge-kyo and urge others to do the same; that will remain as the only memory of your present life in this human world" (WND-1, 64). As these words indicate, practicing ourselves and teaching others to do the same are actions that produce the greatest possible good.

Buddhahood Lies in Our Dedication to the Great Vow for Kosen-rufu

The "great vow" refers to the propagation of the Lotus Sutra. (OTT, 82)

The heartfelt wish of Shakyamuni, the founder of Buddhism, was for all people to become happy. In "Expedient Means," the Lotus Sutra's second chapter, he states, "At the start I took a vow, hoping to make all persons equal to me, without any distinction between us" (LSOC, 70). His vow was to elevate all people to the same enlightened life state he enjoyed.

Nichiren Daishonin was committed to leading all people in the Latter Day of the Law to enlightenment. Embodying the spirit conveyed by his declaration "Not once have I thought of retreat" (WND-2, 465), he overcame every conceivable hardship to spread the Mystic Law. In doing so, he opened the great path by which we can attain the same life state as the Buddha, without any distinction between us and him.

In *The Twenty-Six Admonitions of Nikko*, Nichiren's direct disciple and successor instructs, "Until kosen-rufu is achieved, propagate the Law to the full extent of your ability without begrudging your life" (GZ, 1618). Those who dedicate themselves to kosen-rufu are the Daishonin's true disciples and successors in faith.

The Soka Gakkai has developed dynamically as a world religion precisely because its members have striven tirelessly to spread the Mystic Law just as the Daishonin teaches, devoting themselves diligently to practice for both themselves and others.

Realizing Happiness in Our Daily Lives

In the midst of his life-threatening exile on Sado Island, Nichiren composed "The Opening of the Eyes" and declared, "Here I will make a great vow" (WND-1, 280). He vowed to be the pillar, the eyes, and the great ship that would lead all people to enlightenment, his sole wish being the realization of kosen-rufu.

As the above passage says, "The 'great vow' refers to the propagation of the Lotus Sutra." It is none other than the great vow for kosen-rufu. This is identical to the vow of the Bodhisattvas of the Earth.

Day after day, SGI members chant Nam-myoho-renge-kyo to the Gohonzon and engage in dialogue for the happiness of themselves and others. In this troubled age of the Latter Day, they uphold the great vow for kosen-rufu as they carry out bodhisattva practice all around the globe.

Mr. Makiguchi declared that Buddhism is a teaching for daily life. It is a teaching that enables us to make the most of our lives. We are invigorating ourselves and others every day through our efforts to share Buddhism. Through dialogue, the most basic means of engaging with others, we impart the light of hope and renewal to those who have lost their way in life, are in the depths of suffering, or are unable to find any meaning in living. In the process, together with them, we elevate our appreciation for the meaning of life itself. This is indeed the noble practice of contributing to a revolutionary transformation in the life state of all humanity.

A Cornerstone in Efforts to Build World Peace

The SGI is the organization acting in accord with the Buddha's intent. It has stood up in modern times with a commitment to realize the great vow for kosen-rufu, in perfect harmony with the spirit of Nichiren Daishonin. It is the only organization advancing worldwide kosen-rufu; it is the organization actively dedicated to spreading the Mystic Law.

Spreading the Mystic Law, sharing it with others, spreads waves of joy.

Mr. Toda said: "Sharing Buddhism shouldn't be something painful or unpleasant. It should be done with joy." Altruistic bodhisattva practice always brims with the joy of creating value based on our vow for kosen-rufu.

In November 2013, for the opening of the Hall of the Great Vow for Kosen-rufu, I sent a message to our members, which reads in part: "The heart of the great vow for kosen-rufu and the life state of Buddhahood are one and the same. When we remain true to this vow, the limitless courage, wisdom, and compassion of the Buddha flow forth from within us. As such, when we wholeheartedly strive to realize this vow, the 'poison' of even the most difficult challenge can be transformed into 'medicine,' and karma transformed into mission."

More and more members, Bodhisattvas of the Earth dedicated to fulfilling the great vow for kosen-rufu, are emerging all around the world. They are carrying out bodhisattva practice in their respective countries, leading many people to the path of happiness. Through dialogue, they are building a network of people that transcends national boundaries. By its very existence, the SGI has become a cornerstone in efforts to build world peace.

Thoughtful and aware individuals around the globe have the highest hopes for the SGI, whose members are expanding a network of happiness and peace based on a philosophy of inner human revolution.

Dr. Anatol Rapoport, a former professor of Peace and Conflict Studies at the University of Toronto in Canada, once said: "While many of the world's peace movements are inspired by a fear of nuclear weapons and war, the SGI's peace movement operates at a more profound level, deriving from members' positive conviction that peace means the realization of joy and happiness for all. In that respect, the SGI is unique among the world's peace organizations."[26]

The Noble Bodhisattva Way of Soka

A bright, expansive future lies ahead of us. We are moving toward our next important milestone—the fifth anniversary of the completion of the Hall of the Great Vow for Kosen-rufu in November 2018. That will be followed by the ninetieth anniversary of the Soka Gakkai in 2020, and its one hundredth anniversary in 2030.

Let's continue to advance together with our fellow members around the world, one in heart and mind, always moving forward, our sights set on the next mountaintop. The SGI is an organization of action. Our continual effort is the key to our movement's development and success.

Our activities as Bodhisattvas of the Earth to encourage others and to work for the happiness of ourselves and others are the ultimate forms of bodhisattva practice. We, the members of the Soka family, are a magnificent force of Bodhisattvas of the Earth that will shine eternally in the history of the people.

With pride in pursuing the noble bodhisattva way of Soka, let's strive diligently in our practice for ourselves and others and together lead glorious, triumphant lives!

THREE

The Buddhist Study
of the Soka Gakkai:

Elevating People's Life State

What is the purpose of religion? It is to realize happiness for ourselves and others, the happiness of all people, and to bring about peace in the world.

To achieve that goal, each person must become wise and strong. That was the unshakable conviction of Soka Gakkai founding president Tsunesaburo Makiguchi.

What is good? What is the correct path in life? These are universal questions that have occupied human beings from time immemorial. Mr. Makiguchi sought and found in Nichiren's Buddhism of the Sun, in Nichiren's writings, a solid, life-affirming philosophy that could wisely guide people in answering these questions.

November 18 is the anniversary of the Soka Gakkai's founding (in 1930), and also the day (in 1944) that Mr. Makiguchi died in prison for his beliefs. To the very end, he refused to be defeated by the oppression of Japan's militarist government, and he remained committed to the cause of helping all people realize genuine happiness.

When he was imprisoned, the first thing he asked for was a copy of Nichiren's writings. Even though the harsh prison conditions and meager meals took their toll on the elderly Mr. Makiguchi, his seeking spirit continued to burn brightly.

In letters he sent to his family from prison, he wrote: "Faith is most important,"[27] "[I am] concentrating utterly on faith,"[28] and "What I am going through is nothing compared to the hardships endured by the Daishonin on Sado."[29] His words overflowed with the pride of living based on faith and the Daishonin's writings, even if it should mean giving his life.

His disciple Josei Toda, imprisoned at the same time, also persevered with unwavering commitment. He continued to read Nichiren's writings and the Lotus Sutra, steadily chant Nam-myoho-renge-kyo, and engage in deep contemplation, finally awakening to the truth that the Buddha is life itself and realizing that he was a Bodhisattva of the Earth.

For the sake of human happiness and world peace, both Mr. Makiguchi and Mr. Toda fought resolutely against the devilish nature of authority. Even in prison, they solemnly and dauntlessly exerted themselves in the "two ways of practice and study" (WND-1, 386). This spirit of selfless dedication to propagating the Law, of striving ceaselessly for kosen-rufu, is one that I have also inherited. It is the very heart of the mentor-disciple spirit linking the first three Soka Gakkai presidents.

For both Mr. Makiguchi and Mr. Toda, reading the Daishonin's writings was an inseparable part of their wholehearted struggle to embody the life state of Buddhahood. Their spirit of deeply taking to heart and actualizing the Daishonin's writings through their actions continues to live on in the SGI today. The SGI has built a great philosophical movement that is based on a spirit of self-reliance and self-motivation. It is a movement in which ordinary people study Buddhism, share it with others, and personally put it into practice.

This "university without walls," where the people develop and train themselves through Buddhist practice and study, has now spread around the world. In this chapter, let us explore the spirit of Buddhist study shared by Soka mentors and disciples.

Reading the Daishonin's Writings
As If They Were Addressed to Us Directly

There is very little writing paper here in the province of Sado, and to write to you individually would take too long. Nevertheless, if even one person fails to hear from me, it will cause resentment. Therefore, I want people with seeking minds to meet and read this letter together for encouragement. (WND-I, 306)

The majority of Nichiren's letters to his disciples were composed after he was exiled to Sado Island, and more particularly, after he moved to Mount Minobu—that is, a time when it was difficult for him to meet with them in person.

His letters express his great compassion; they brim with concern and sensitivity for the feelings of his disciples who were facing harsh persecution, grieving over the loss of loved ones, or were weighed down by life's hardships. Precisely because his letters are filled with heartwarming, life-to-life exchanges with his disciples, they transcend the ages and can move readers deeply even today.

Nichiren wrote the above passage in "Letter from Sado" at a time when his life was being threatened. Because of a shortage of paper, he set down his thoughts and feelings in a single letter to be shared with all of his disciples.

Gathering in small groups to read or listen to this letter during a time of raging persecution, they must have been profoundly moved by the Daishonin's warm concern for them. His towering state of life, his spirit to strive for kosen-rufu fully prepared to meet with any persecution, must have filled his disciples with courage. I can imagine that, after hearing the letter read, they vowed together to remain steadfast in faith, encouraging one another, and setting forth with fresh resolve.

We, too, can experience this same beautiful mentor-disciple communication today. It is important for us to read Nichiren's writings with the spirit that they are addressed personally to each one of us, that he is speaking to us directly.

Persevering in Buddhist Study in the Midst of Hardships

In Mr. Makiguchi's copy of the collected writings of Nichiren, many passages in "The Opening of the Eyes" are underlined in red and the margins are filled with notes, such as "Propagation," "Great vow," and "What is the mark of a genuine practitioner?" These notes reflect his solemn spirit to seek the way of Buddhist practice.

He once said, "I cannot read the Daishonin's writings without being moved to tears by his great compassion." As

Mr. Makiguchi's words suggest, the whole point of reading the Daishonin's writings is to connect with the Daishonin's spirit.

Describing his emotions on reading a passage from "The Opening of the Eyes" and connecting with the Daishonin's passion and life force, Mr. Toda once wrote: "His blazing spirit strikes my heart with the intensity of the noonday summer sun. My chest feels as if it is filled with a giant ball of molten iron. Sometimes I feel like a scalding spring is gushing forth inside me, or as if a great, earthshaking waterfall is crashing over me."[30]

I recall that in my youth, as I strove to assist Mr. Toda during great troubles, I read Nichiren's writings every day, no matter how exhausted I was.

In my diary from those times, I expressed my joy at reading them: "Where shall sensitive youth turn for an answer? As I read [Nichiren's writings], I tremble with delight. Buddhism, clearly expounding the origin and basis of all, offering true happiness."[31]

Mr. Makiguchi said: "You should not seek to understand Buddhism with your mind. You come to understand it through faith." In other words, even if we may find the teachings of Buddhism difficult to understand, through an earnest desire and commitment to learn about and deepen our grasp of them in the course of our efforts for kosen-rufu, we will be able to elevate our state of life.

By reading Nichiren's writings every day, even just a sentence or short passage, we can make our lives shine brilliantly.

Reading Nichiren's Writings
When We Reach an Impasse

When we are in the depths of despair, reading Nichiren's writings can make the sun of hope rise in our hearts. When we face an impasse, reading them can help us summon forth the fearless spirit of a lion king. And when suffering from illness, reading them can fill our lives with reinvigorating vitality.

In the early days of our organization, members always carried a copy of Nichiren's writings with them as they engaged in propagation efforts, personal guidance, and other activities for kosen-rufu. Before or after gongyo at meetings, they would read passages from the Daishonin's writings aloud.

Their copies of Nichiren's writings, which were always with them through good times and bad, were worn and tattered from use and full of underlining and notes. The members made it through each day by reading and engaging with Nichiren's writings.

To engrave the Daishonin's writings in one's heart, to bring forth the invincible life state of Buddhahood, and to advance toward fulfilling the great vow for kosen-rufu while struggling with one's karma—this is the path of Buddhist study that leads directly to a life of happiness and victory.

Imbuing Our Lives With Buddhahood

> One who, on hearing the teachings of the
> Lotus Sutra, makes even greater efforts in faith
> is a true seeker of the way. T'ien-t'ai states,
> "From the indigo, an even deeper blue." This
> passage means that, if one dyes something
> repeatedly in indigo, it becomes even bluer
> than the indigo leaves. The Lotus Sutra is like
> the indigo, and the strength of one's practice is
> like the deepening blue. (WND-1, 457)

This passage is from "Hell Is the Land of Tranquil Light," a letter addressed to the lay nun Ueno, who, while still grieving over the death of her husband, was working hard to raise her children on her own.

In the letter, Nichiren empathizes with her grief and warmly encourages her, praying that she will overcome her sadness and find happiness. The lay nun Ueno had striven in her Buddhist practice with pure and steadfast faith. But when her husband died, leaving her alone to care for their family, she must at times have been filled with despair.

The Daishonin explained to her the Buddhist teaching of the enlightenment of the dragon king's daughter,[32] who in the Lotus Sutra attains Buddhahood in her present form.[33] By doing so, he infused her heart with the light of hope that she could become happy without fail.

To attain Buddhahood in one's present form, one must dispel the fundamental ignorance[34] that obscures the potential for Buddhahood. The key is to "make even greater efforts in faith."

The struggle between the Buddha and devilish functions within our own lives is not an easy one to win. To beat devilish functions, we have to make unceasing efforts to chant Nam-myoho-renge-kyo and teach others to do the same, strengthening and deepening our faith.

In this letter, the Daishonin uses the metaphor of "bluer than indigo itself"[35] to describe the process of deepening our faith. Exerting ourselves in our Buddhist practice day after day to realize our wishes strengthens our prayers and deepens our faith. Reading Nichiren's writings does the same. By reading them again and again as we strive forward, his courage and justice, his boundless compassion, and above all, his passionate commitment to propagating the Mystic Law will be etched in our lives. In this way, we imbue, or "dye," our lives with Buddhahood. As he assures us in another letter, "Those who are imbued with the Lotus Sutra [Nam-myoho-renge-kyo] will invariably become Buddhas" (WND-2, 675).

When we persevere in our Buddhist practice, seeking to connect with the Daishonin's state of life and to deepen our conviction that we are Bodhisattvas of the Earth and embodiments of the Mystic Law, we can attain a state of absolute happiness in which being alive is itself the greatest joy.

Tapping the Inexhaustible Benefit of the Gohonzon With the Power of Faith

When Mr. Toda was rebuilding the Soka Gakkai after World War II, he often said the reason that the other top Soka Gakkai leaders quit the organization when they were arrested by the wartime militarist authorities was that they lacked a foundation of Buddhist study. After the war, he devoted himself wholeheartedly to promoting the study of Nichiren Buddhism to foster disciples who would remain undaunted in the face of any opposition.

Addressing members who didn't feel the need for Buddhist study, Mr. Toda said:

I hear that some of you say, "As long as I can receive benefit, I'm happy; I don't care about studying Buddhism." That's absurd. Buddhist study strengthens and increases your faith, which produces benefit.

Nichiren Buddhism teaches the four powers.[36] The power of the Buddha and the power of the Law increase in proportion to the strength of the power of faith and the power of practice. Therefore, bringing forth the powers of the Buddha and the Law in your life depends on the powers of your own faith and practice. The latter merge to become the powers of the Buddha and the Law, resulting in benefits that seem miraculous, defying comprehension.[37]

It is the power of faith that enables us to freely tap the great and inexhaustible benefit of the Gohonzon. And Buddhist study is the means by which we strengthen our power of faith.

By deepening our understanding of Nichiren Buddhism, our questions and doubts give way to clarity, which in turn intensifies our prayers. When we truly come to understand how wonderful this Buddhism is, our prayers will be filled with gratitude. When we have unshakable conviction that our desires will be fulfilled, our prayers will overflow with joy.

That is, by strengthening our faith through Buddhist study, our prayers will be filled with gratitude and joy, enabling us to freely tap the benefit of the Gohonzon.

A Seeking Spirit Is the Direct Path to Happiness and Victory

At lectures he gave at the Toshima Civic Hall, Mr. Toda would often say to the effect, "Supposing the benefit I have received is comparable in size to this hall, then the benefit all of you have received is still no more than the size of my little finger."

He wanted every Soka Gakkai member to experience the infinite benefit of the Gohonzon. It was his sincerest wish that each person become happy. As his disciple, sharing his spirit and commitment, I have given lectures with the same wish.

Having a seeking mind is crucial in Buddhist study. Being a person who has admirable, strong faith is not a matter of simply having a great deal of knowledge. Rather, it's a matter of striving earnestly for kosen-rufu, always based on the Daishonin's spirit.

There is no final goal on the path of study. The more we study, the more we deepen not only our understanding but also our faith and practice. When we persevere sincerely in faith, always moving forward and improving ourselves, we will enjoy a state of life of limitless freedom as "true seekers of the way" (see WND-1, 457).

That is also the purpose of our SGI activities.

When we are dealing with problems and difficulties, we may sometimes feel heavyhearted and reluctant to attend SGI meetings. But those are precisely the times that our lives can be energized by making an effort to attend these gatherings of Buddhas, studying the Daishonin's teachings, and listening to others' experiences. This is the way to polish our faith, expand our state of life, and set forth again with light hearts and renewed vigor.

Members Studying Around the World

> Exert yourself in the two ways of practice and study. Without practice and study, there can be no Buddhism. You must not only persevere yourself; you must also teach others. Both practice and study arise from faith. Teach others to the best of your ability, even if it is only a single sentence or phrase. (WND-1, 386)

This passage from "The True Aspect of All Phenomena" is one that we should all engrave in our hearts as practitioners of Nichiren Buddhism.

In his copy of Nichiren's writings, Mr. Makiguchi marked for special attention the page containing this passage about "the two ways of practice and study."

Mr. Toda also cited this passage in his foreword to the Soka Gakkai edition of the *Nichiren Daishonin Gosho zenshu* (The collected writings of Nichiren Daishonin), and wrote:

Since its establishment by our first president, Tsunesaburo Makiguchi, the Soka Gakkai has treasured these words of Nichiren Daishonin and, persevering in "the two ways of study and practice" based on pure and strong faith, has engaged energetically in efforts to propagate the Mystic Law just as the Buddha teaches. This rigorous training, comparable to the training of a master swordsman, has become the tradition and proud hallmark of the Soka Gakkai.

The SGI has kept the solemn and sublime spirit of the Daishonin alive by advancing steadfastly based on the "two ways of practice and study."

Mr. Toda concludes his foreword by saying, "It is my undying wish and prayer that this precious and unparalleled scripture be spread throughout all of Asia and the entire world."

Today, Nichiren's writings have been translated into more than ten languages and is being studied by members in 192 countries and territories. That it has transmitted the Daishonin's writings throughout the world is clear proof that the SGI is making the global propagation of Nichiren Buddhism a reality. How delighted Mr. Toda would surely be to see this!

Given the very different times in which the Daishonin lived and the culture and customs amid which he wrote, unfamiliar to most non-Japanese readers, the work of translating Nichiren's writings is extremely challenging. It is being carried out through the efforts of modern-day Kumarajivas[38] around the world. They are translating the Daishonin's writings for the sake of worldwide kosen-rufu and the future of humanity. To do so, they tirelessly seek to deepen their understanding of his spirit and pray earnestly to be able to accurately convey his message to others. I would like to sincerely thank them for their noble, dedicated efforts to open the doors of worldwide kosen-rufu.

Nichiren's writings are filled with teachings of hope, which the Daishonin presented to all humanity. They overflow with the great compassion to lead all people to enlightenment and resound with a lion's roar for truth and justice. They have limitless power to inspire and encourage and revitalize people's lives.

Practice and Study Are the Heart of Buddhism

The Daishonin writes: "Without practice and study, there can be no Buddhism. You must not only persevere yourself; you must also teach others." Practice and study—which we carry out ourselves and encourage others to do as well—are the heart of Buddhism. In Nichiren Buddhism, it isn't enough that we practice for our own happiness alone. There is no such thing as a selfish Buddha satisfied with attaining personal enlightenment and caring nothing for anyone else. The wisdom of the Buddha exists to lead all people to happiness.

Mr. Makiguchi and Mr. Toda's efforts in practice and study while in prison clearly demonstrate that the Soka Gakkai is directly connected to Nichiren Daishonin. The Soka Gakkai is an organization eternally dedicated to Buddhist study put into action, just as this passage teaches.

A Philosophy for Transforming Our Lives

The Daishonin continues: "Both practice and study arise from faith. Teach others to the best of your ability, even if it is only a single sentence or phrase." Faith is expressed as concrete efforts in practice and study.

"To the best of your ability" means exerting yourself to the fullest. There is no need to feel hesitant about talking to others about Buddhism because you're not good at Buddhist study. For instance, you could just share some of Nichiren's words that you find moving or something you learned through your Buddhist practice. Or you can tell someone, even with just a few words, that practicing Nichiren Buddhism is enjoyable, that it will enable them to make their wishes come true.

Mr. Toda said:

Buddhist study in the Soka Gakkai entails reading Nichiren's writings with our deeds, words, and thoughts.[39] As the Daishonin quotes, "The voice carries out the work of the Buddha" (OTT, 4). Please talk with others freely and unhesitatingly about what you've learned about Nichiren Buddhism. By doing so, Buddhist study will eventually become part of your life.

He also said, "Simply attending lectures or reading the Daishonin's writings and saying that one understands the teachings is still the realm of theory; the important thing is to exert oneself in faith and practice in accord with those teachings."

He further stressed to us that actually transforming our lives is more important than mere understanding.

Study based on the mentor-disciple spirit is the Soka Gakkai tradition. It is study for winning, providing us with the foundation to overcome obstacles by learning from Nichiren's conduct and summoning forth the spirit of a lion king. It is study for deepening our faith. It is study for sharing the Mystic Law and realizing kosen-rufu, which spurs us to talk to others about the inspiration and joy we gain from studying the Daishonin's teachings. It is study for inner transformation and human revolution, providing us an opportunity to connect with the Daishonin's heart and confirm that we ourselves embody the Mystic Law.

Practice and study arise from faith, and faith is deepened by pursuing "the two ways of practice and study." This is the rhythm of human revolution and kosen-rufu.

An "Indestructible Axle"

Just before this passage about the "two ways of practice and study," the Daishonin declares, "Believe in the Gohonzon, the supreme object of devotion in all of Jambudvipa [the entire world]" (WND-1, 386). Nichiren inscribed the Gohonzon to enable all people to attain Buddhahood. With absolute faith in the Gohonzon as its driving force, the SGI has been working to realize worldwide kosen-rufu.

The Soka Gakkai Kosen-rufu Gohonzon,[40] enshrined in the Hall of the Great Vow for Kosen-rufu in Shinanomachi, Tokyo, is the Gohonzon that Mr. Toda requested to be inscribed as an "indestructible axle" for the progress of our Soka movement. He made the request just after he announced his goal of a membership of 750,000 households (in May 1951).

The Soka Gakkai thus began a great advance, directly connected to Nichiren Daishonin and based on the "two wheels" of practice and study united through absolute faith in this great "indestructible axle."

As an organization carrying out the Buddha's intent, the SGI will without fail achieve "kosen-rufu through the compassionate propagation of the great Law," which is the great vow and desire of Nichiren Daishonin! In accord with this vow, in Mr. Toda's lifetime, we realized the goal of a membership of 750,000 households, and in the time since, during which I have devoted myself as his disciple, we have spread the Mystic Law to 192 countries and territories.

Nothing can stop the advance of our Soka movement, which is based on faith, practice, and study and permeated by this great vow of mentor and disciple.

Open the Door to Happiness for Humanity

Nichiren Buddhism focuses on the present and future.

Faith, practice, and study are the fundamental guidelines for expanding our state of life. They compose the hope-filled formula for shaping our own destiny and building a path of eternal happiness.

The German composer Ludwig van Beethoven endured the loss of his hearing and transcended that painful destiny to bring joy to humanity. It is recorded that "he [often] spoke of the duty which was imposed on him to act by means of his art 'for poor humanity, for humanity to come, to restore its courage and to shake off its lassitude and cowardice.'"[41]

Our destiny is to live as proud SGI members and fulfill our mission as Bodhisattvas of the Earth. It is to dedicate our lives to kosen-rufu, which is building happiness for the entire human race.

With our ceaseless efforts in faith, practice, and study, let us cast off the iron fetters of karma holding us down!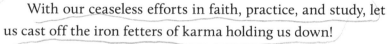

With the vibrant energy of our faith, practice, and study, let us spread joy around the world and elevate people's life state!

With the golden basics of faith, practice, and study, let us open even more powerfully the doors to the eternal victory and prosperity of our Soka movement!

NOTES

Chapter One—The Faith of the Soka Gakkai:
Unlocking Immeasurable Good Fortune and Benefit

1. Translated from Japanese: Josei Toda, *Toda Josei zenshu* (The collected writings of Josei Toda) (Tokyo: Seikyo Shimbunsha, 1983), 3:72.

2. *Josei Toda zenshu*, 3:72–73.

3. The Japanese word for *faith* consists of two Chinese characters.

4. Translated from Japanese. Josei Toda, *Toda Josei zenshu* (The collected writings of Josei Toda) (Tokyo: Seikyo Shimbunsha, 1984), 4:582.

5. *Josei Toda zenshu*, 4:583.

6. This passage teaches that the Buddha appears in response to this single-minded seeking spirit. This may be interpreted as awakening to the eternal world of Buddhahood within one's own life. In other words, the life state of Buddhahood emerges in those who tirelessly devote themselves to realizing the great vow for kosen-rufu with unwavering seeking spirit toward the Buddha and faith in the Mystic Law.

7. Translated from Japanese. Josei Toda, *Toda Josei zenshu* (The collected writings of Josei Toda) (Tokyo: Seikyo Shimbunsha, 1981), 1:149.

8. LSOC, 79.

9. LSOC, 115.

10. Tatsunokuchi Persecution: The failed attempt, instigated by powerful government figures, to behead Nichiren Daishonin under the cover of darkness on the beach at Tatsunokuchi, on the outskirts of Kamakura, on September 12, 1271.

11. Buddha of the Latter Day of the Law: The Buddha of the Latter Day of the Law is an ordinary person and an ordinary priest. "An ordinary priest" here refers to Nichiren. Because Nichiren revealed and spread Nam-myoho-renge-kyo, which is manifest as the Person and the Law, he is regarded by his disciple and designated successor Nikko and his followers as the Buddha of the Latter Day of the Law.

12. In "King Rinda," the Daishonin writes that when King Rinda heard the white horses neighing, "[His] complexion was restored to its original state, like the sun reemerging from an eclipse, and the strength of his body and the perceptive powers of his mind became many hundreds and thousands of times greater than they had been before" (WND-1, 986).

13. Translated from Japanese. Josei Toda, *Toda Josei zenshu* (The collected writings of Josei Toda) (Tokyo: Seikyo Shimbunsha, 1982), 2:467.

14. See *Josei Toda zenshu*, 2:466–67.

Chapter Two—The Practice of the Soka Gakkai: Carrying Out Bodhisattva Practice in the Present Day

15. M. K. Gandhi, *My Religion,* comp. and ed. Bharatan Kumarappa (Ahmedabad: Navajivan Publishing House, 1958), 51.

16. First step for worldwide kosen-rufu: President Ikeda took his first trip outside of Japan in October 1960, just five months after becoming president. He has since visited more than

fifty countries to spread the SGI's ideals of peace, culture, and education.

17. Composed in 1255, "On Attaining Buddhahood in This Lifetime" (WND-I, 3–4) teaches that chanting Nam-myoho-renge-kyo is the direct path to attaining Buddhahood in this lifetime.

18. Translated from Japanese. Tsunesaburo Makiguchi, *Makiguchi Tsunesaburo zenshu* (The collected writings of Tsunesaburo Makiguchi) (Tokyo: Daisanbunmei-sha, 1987), 10:151.

19. Fundamental ignorance or darkness: The most deeply rooted illusion inherent in life, said to give rise to all other illusions. The inability to see or recognize the truth, particularly, the true nature of one's life.

20. In the Lotus Sutra, the world in which we dwell is described as a place "where living beings enjoy themselves at ease." This indicates that the saha world, normally regarded as a realm of suffering, is actually the Land of Eternally Tranquil Light, or a Buddha realm, where all living beings can experience the greatest enjoyment.

21. Composed in 1279, "Letter to Jakunichi-bo" (WND-I, 993–94) is addressed to one of the Daishonin's disciples thought to have been resident in Awa Province (presently, part of Chiba Prefecture), sent via a disciple named Jakunichi-bo.

22. Three poisons of greed, anger, and foolishness: The fundamental evils inherent in life that give rise to human suffering. In the renowned Mahayana scholar Nagarjuna's *Treatise on the Great Perfection of Wisdom,* the three poisons are regarded as the source of all illusions and earthly desires. The three poisons are so called because they pollute people's lives and work to prevent them from turning their hearts and minds to goodness.

23. Twenty-line verse section: The concluding verse section of "Encouraging Devotion," the Lotus Sutra's thirteenth chapter, in which countless multitudes of bodhisattvas vow to Shakyamuni Buddha to propagate the sutra in the evil age after his passing,

enduring the attacks of the three powerful enemies: arrogant lay people, arrogant priests, and arrogant false sages. It is called the twenty-line verse section because the Chinese translation consists of twenty lines.

24. Bodhisattva Superior Practices: The leader of the Bodhisattvas of the Earth who appear in "Emerging from the Earth," the Lotus Sutra's fifteenth chapter. In the twenty-first chapter, "Supernatural Powers," Shakyamuni entrusts Superior Practices with propagating the Lotus Sutra during the evil age of the Latter Day of the Law.

25. The Daishonin writes: "The [Lotus Sutra] reads, 'As the light of the sun and moon can banish all obscurity and gloom, so this person as he advances through the world can wipe out the darkness of living beings' [LSOC, 318]. Consider carefully what this passage signifies. 'This person as he advances through the world' means that the first five hundred years of the Latter Day of the Law will witness the advent of Bodhisattva Superior Practices, who will illuminate the darkness of ignorance and earthly desires with the light of the five characters of Nam-myoho-renge-kyo. In accordance with this passage, Nichiren, as this bodhisattva's envoy, has urged the people of Japan to accept and uphold the Lotus Sutra. His unremitting efforts never slacken, even here on this mountain [of Minobu]" (WND-1, 993).

26. Translated from Japanese. From an article about the activities of SGI-Canada in the July 7, 2001, *Seikyo Shimbun*.

Chapter Three—The Buddhist Study of the Soka Gakkai: Elevating People's Life State

27. Translated from Japanese. Tsunesaburo Makiguchi, *Makiguchi Tsunesaburo zenshu* (The collected writings of Tsunesaburo Makiguchi) (Tokyo: Daisanbunmei-sha, 1987), 10:278.

28. *Tsunesaburo Makiguchi zenshu*, 10:276

29. *Tsunesaburo Makiguchi zenshu*, 10:282.

30. Translated from Japanese. Josei Toda, *Toda Josei zenshu* (The collected writings of Josei Toda) (Tokyo: Seikyo Shimbunsha, 1983), 3:179.

31. Daisaku Ikeda, *A Youthful Diary: One Man's Journey From the Beginning of Faith to Worldwide Leadership for Peace* (Santa Monica, CA: World Tribune Press, 2006), 5.

32. Dragon king's daughter: Also, the dragon girl. The eight-year-old daughter of Sagara, one of the eight great dragon kings said to dwell in a palace at the bottom of the sea. According to "Devadatta," the Lotus Sutra's twelfth chapter, the dragon girl conceives the desire for enlightenment upon hearing Bodhisattva Manjushri preach the Lotus Sutra in the dragon king's palace. She then appears in front of the assembly of the Lotus Sutra and, declaring "I unfold the doctrines of the great vehicle to rescue living beings from suffering" (LSOC, 227), instantaneously attains Buddhahood in her present form. The dragon girl's enlightenment is a model for the enlightenment of women and reveals the power of the Lotus Sutra to enable all people equally to attain Buddhahood just as they are.

33. Attaining Buddhahood in one's present form: This means attaining Buddhahood in this lifetime just as one is, without undergoing endless eons of Buddhist practice.

34. Fundamental ignorance or darkness: The most deeply rooted illusion inherent in life, said to give rise to all other illusions. The inability to see or recognize the truth, particularly, the true nature of one's life.

35. The simile "becoming bluer than the indigo" derives from a writing of the Chinese philosopher Hsün Tzu. The juice extracted from the indigo plant is used as a dye. Although the juice is not a deep blue itself, cloth dipped in it is dyed blue. Repeated dyeing produces ever deeper shades. As such, the simile refers to deepening one's learning through study.

36. The four powers: The power of the Buddha, the power of the Law, the power of faith, and the power of practice. In Nichiren Buddhism, the four powers are known as the four powers of the Mystic Law, whose interaction enables one to have one's prayers answered and attain Buddhahood. The power of the Buddha is the Buddha's compassion in saving all people. The power of the Law indicates the boundless capacity of the Mystic Law to lead all people to enlightenment. The power of faith is to believe in the Gohonzon, the object of devotion that embodies the power of the Buddha and the power of the Law, and the power of practice is to chant Nam-myoho-renge-kyo oneself and teach others to do the same. To the extent that one brings forth one's powers of faith and practice, one can manifest the powers of the Buddha and the Law within one's own life.

37. Translated from Japanese. Josei Toda, *Toda Josei zenshu* (The collected writings of Josei Toda) (Tokyo: Seikyo Shimbunsha, 1989), 4:42.

38. Kumarajiva (344–413): Translator of the Lotus Sutra into Chinese. Nichiren, as did many others, prized his translation for its excellence and clarity.

39. This refers to the three categories of action; also, three types of action. Activities carried out with one's body, mouth, and mind, i.e., deeds, words, and thoughts. Buddhism holds that karma, good or evil, is created by these three types of action—mental, verbal, and physical. Here, "action" is the translation of the Sanskrit *karman*.

40. In addition to the inscription "For the Fulfillment of the Great Vow for Kosen-rufu Through the Compassionate Propagation of the Great Law," the Gohonzon enshrined in the Hall of the Great Vow for Kosen-rufu also bears the inscription "To Be Permanently Enshrined for the Soka Gakkai" (Jpn *Soka Gakkai Joju*).

41. Romain Rolland, *Beethoven,* trans. B. Constance Hull (London: Kegan Paul, Trench, Trubner and Co., Ltd., 1919), 49.